HAPPINESS FOR EVERY DAY

An Hachette UK Company
www.hachette.co.uk

Summersdale Publishers Ltd
Part of Octopus Publishing Group Limited
Carmelite House
50 Victoria Embankment
LONDON
EC4Y 0DZ
UK

www.summersdale.com

Printed and bound in China

ISBN: 978-1-78783-652-5

Substantial discounts on bulk quantities of Summersdale books are available to corporations, professional associations and other organizations. For details contact general enquiries: telephone: +44 (0) 1243 771107 or email: enquiries@summersdale.com.

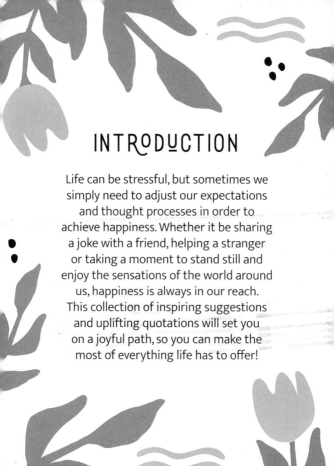

INTRODUCTION

Life can be stressful, but sometimes we simply need to adjust our expectations and thought processes in order to achieve happiness. Whether it be sharing a joke with a friend, helping a stranger or taking a moment to stand still and enjoy the sensations of the world around us, happiness is always in our reach. This collection of inspiring suggestions and uplifting quotations will set you on a joyful path, so you can make the most of everything life has to offer!

SIMPLE PLEASURES ARE THE BEST

Savour the everyday things that you enjoy. Focus on anything you like – hugging your pet, drinking a refreshing juice or smelling the food you are about to eat. Give yourself time to notice these agreeable things and life becomes full of small pleasures.

WEALTH CONSISTS
NOT IN HAVING GREAT
POSSESSIONS, BUT IN
HAVING FEW WANTS.

Epictetus

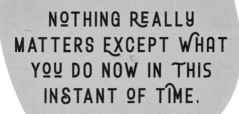

NOTHING REALLY
MATTERS EXCEPT WHAT
YOU DO NOW IN THIS
INSTANT OF TIME.

Eileen Caddy

START THE DAY WELL

Begin each day with a positive morning routine. Allow yourself time for meditation (or at least a moment of reflection), a healthy breakfast and some exercise. You can then move into your day calm and happy.

HAPPINESS MUST BE GROWN
IN ONE'S OWN GARDEN.

Mary Engelbreit

TRUE HAPPINESS IS
AN INNER POWER –
NATURAL, HEALING,
ABUNDANT AND
ALWAYS AVAILABLE.

Robert Holden

COME FLY WITH ME

Sit down and plan a trip to a destination you have always dreamed of. Even if it may not happen for years, or at all, it is an uplifting and exciting way to while away a few hours. Who knows, the dream may eventually become a reality!

LAUGHTER IS AN INSTANT VACATION.

Milton Berle

WITH THE NEW
DAY COMES NEW
STRENGTH AND
NEW THOUGHTS.

Eleanor Roosevelt

CHANGE YOUR LANGUAGE

Change your words and you will change your feelings. Replace "I have to do it" with "I want to do it." This creates an energetic shift and enables you to feel more empowered. Try it any time you hear yourself thinking "I have to" or "I should".

HAPPINESS DEPENDS
UPON OURSELVES.

Aristotle

LIFE ISN'T ABOUT
FINDING YOURSELF.
LIFE IS ABOUT
CREATING YOURSELF.

George Bernard Shaw

IT'S PLAYTIME!

Make time to play! It could be football
in the garden or a card game by the
fireside. Have good old-fashioned
fun and enjoy smiles all round.

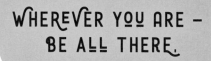

WHEREVER YOU ARE —
BE ALL THERE.

Jim Elliot

HAPPINESS COMES WHEN
YOUR WORK AND WORDS
ARE OF BENEFIT TO
YOURSELF AND OTHERS.

Jack Kornfield

LIVE THE LIFE YOU'VE DREAMED

Remember the dreams you had as a child to travel the world, work with horses or be an actor? If those dreams have not been fulfilled, visualize what passions still remain. How could you manifest a part of your dream into your current life? Perhaps book a trip abroad, go for a horse ride along the seashore or sign up with your local amateur dramatic society.

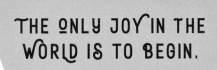

THE ONLY JOY IN THE WORLD IS TO BEGIN.

Cesare Pavese

BUT WHAT IS HAPPINESS
EXCEPT THE SIMPLE
HARMONY BETWEEN A MAN
AND THE LIFE HE LEADS?

Albert Camus

THINK YOURSELF HAPPY

Your brain reacts in the same way whether you are experiencing something that makes you feel happy or just thinking about something happy – both can flood your body with feel-good hormones. This means that you can influence how you feel by what you choose to think. So, think happy!

CHANGE YOUR
THOUGHTS AND YOU
CHANGE YOUR WORLD.

Norman Vincent Peale

IF YOU CARRY JOY IN
YOUR HEART, YOU CAN
HEAL ANY MOMENT.

Carlos Santana

GRATITUDE IS GREAT

Be appreciative of the things others do for you. Buddhist monks call this "watering the flowers of gratitude". Every week, sit down with someone you are close to and tell them all the things you have appreciated about them in the previous days. Let them do the same for you. Practised regularly, this can be a relationship-changer.

ALL THE HAPPINESS
THERE IS IN THIS
WORLD ARISES FROM
WISHING OTHERS
TO BE HAPPY.

Geshe Kelsang Gyatso

LIFE IS A SHIPWRECK, BUT
WE MUST NOT FORGET TO
SING IN THE LIFEBOATS.

Voltaire

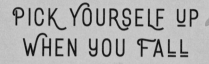

PICK YOURSELF UP WHEN YOU FALL

The word "resilience" stems from the Latin *resilio*, meaning "jump back". In our everyday lives we need to find ways of bouncing back from adversity, to pick ourselves up and carry on. Having supportive friends and managing our behaviour positively are two helpful resilience strategies.

MIX A LITTLE FOOLISHNESS
WITH YOUR SERIOUS PLANS;
IT IS LOVELY TO BE SILLY
AT THE RIGHT MOMENT.

Horace

ACCEPT NO ONE'S
DEFINITION OF
YOUR LIFE; DEFINE
YOURSELF.

Harvey Fierstein

HAVE FUN TOGETHER

The happiest couples are those who spend time together on enjoyable activities. However busy life becomes, make time to share fun – even if you're just exercising, browsing a farmers' market or watching a film. Making time for friends is equally valuable.

IF YOU CAN SOLVE YOUR PROBLEM, THEN WHAT IS THE NEED OF WORRYING? IF YOU CANNOT SOLVE IT, THEN WHAT IS THE USE OF WORRYING?

Śhantideva

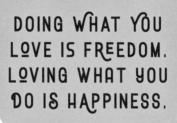

DOING WHAT YOU
LOVE IS FREEDOM.
LOVING WHAT YOU
DO IS HAPPINESS.

Lana Del Rey

FOLLOW YOUR PASSIONS

What are you passionate about?
What energizes you? Which of your
friends do you have the most fun with?
Recognize how you can choose to lift
your spirits by following your heart.

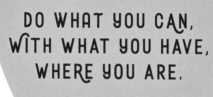

DO WHAT YOU CAN,
WITH WHAT YOU HAVE,
WHERE YOU ARE.

Theodore Roosevelt

THE GREATEST
HAPPINESS IS
TO TRANSFORM
ONE'S FEELINGS
INTO ACTION.

Madame de Staël

LET YOUR THOUGHTS BE THOUGHTS

Humans have over 50,000 thoughts a day, and it's easy to let them dictate how we feel. However, it's important to remember that a thought is just that: a thought. We might not always be able to completely change our emotions, but we can choose not to listen to the kind of thinking that brings us down. Next time you experience a negative thought, allow yourself to acknowledge it, but then let it go.

GO CONFIDENTLY IN THE DIRECTION OF YOUR DREAMS. LIVE THE LIFE YOU'VE IMAGINED.

Henry David Thoreau

BEGIN TO BE NOW
WHAT YOU WILL
BE HEREAFTER.

William James

CREATE A HAPPINESS BOX

Whether it's a shoebox or your bed-side drawer, this is your treasure chest, containing pieces of paper on which you have written moments of happiness. Any time you experience something that has made you smile, filled you with joy, or given you immense satisfaction – write it on some paper, fold it up and place it in your box. You can then take them out and read through all your moments when you want to boost your happiness levels.

ONE JOY SCATTERS
A HUNDRED GRIEFS.

Chinese proverb

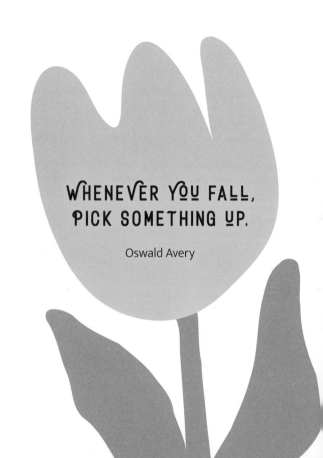

WHENEVER YOU FALL,
PICK SOMETHING UP.

Oswald Avery

WALK ON THE WILD SIDE

Animals have been proven to be natural mood enhancers. By spending time with a pet, you may see a reduction in your stress levels – and they'll provide plenty of reasons for you to laugh and be cheerful! If you don't have a pet, why not pay a visit to a friend or relative who does?

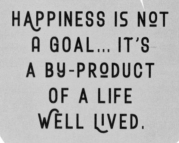

HAPPINESS IS NOT
A GOAL... IT'S
A BY-PRODUCT
OF A LIFE
WELL LIVED.

Eleanor Roosevelt

TURN YOUR FACE TO THE
SUN AND THE SHADOWS
WILL FALL BEHIND YOU.

Maori proverb

BE HERE NOW

Santosa is a Sanskrit word meaning "contentment and acceptance for where we are right now". Allow this beautiful word to enter your vocabulary and let its message brighten your daily life.

RELEASE YOUR STRUGGLE,
LET GO OF YOUR MIND,
THROW AWAY YOUR
CONCERNS, AND RELAX
INTO THE WORLD.

Dan Millman

THE ONLY JOURNEY IS
THE ONE WITHIN.

Rainer Maria Rilke

I LIKE TO
MOVE IT, MOVE IT

Our bodies produce chemicals called
endorphins, which are natural happiness
boosters. When you spend time doing
something you truly enjoy, your
body is flooded with these feel-good
chemicals. So, try to spend some time
on joyful activities every day, from a
quiet walk in the country or a park,
to an exhilarating cycle ride or run.

A SMILE IS A
CURVE THAT SETS
EVERYTHING
STRAIGHT.

Phyllis Diller

IF YOU HAVE GOOD
THOUGHTS THEY WILL
SHINE OUT OF YOUR FACE
LIKE SUNBEAMS AND YOU
WILL ALWAYS LOOK LOVELY.

Roald Dahl

CELEBRATE YOUR GOALS

Be clear about what motivates you. High achievers have been found to have a strong desire be successful, whereas those less accomplished simply wish to avoid failure. You can view demanding tasks as needing dedication and commitment, rather than as overloading and stressful. It's your choice!

LIVE TODAY FOR TOMORROW IT WILL ALL BE HISTORY.

Proverb

DON'T COUNT THE DAYS:
MAKE THE DAYS COUNT.

Muhammad Ali

THE BRIGHT STUFF

Do you have a rainbow of coloured clothes
in your wardrobe? Possibly not, but a
brightly coloured item of clothing can help
you show the world you are happy and
full of life. If you don't have any colourful
clothes, why not treat yourself to some?

KEEP SMILING, BECAUSE LIFE IS A BEAUTIFUL THING AND THERE'S SO MUCH TO SMILE ABOUT.

Marilyn Monroe

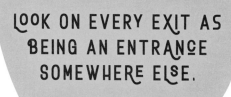

LOOK ON EVERY EXIT AS
BEING AN ENTRANCE
SOMEWHERE ELSE.

Tom Stoppard

ALLOW YOURSELF TO LAUGH

Let go of heaviness – things don't have to be serious all the time. Lighten up with a joke and try to laugh at life's absurdities.

LIFE IS EITHER A DARING
ADVENTURE OR NOTHING.

Helen Keller

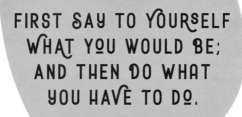

FIRST SAY TO YOURSELF
WHAT YOU WOULD BE;
AND THEN DO WHAT
YOU HAVE TO DO.

Epictetus

GET CREATIVE

Tap into your creativity. Reimagine an area of your living space or simply decorate and add some new touches to a room in your home; take up a brand-new hobby such as watercolour painting, cake decorating or renovating old furniture – anything you feel comfortable with.

THERE ARE ALWAYS
FLOWERS FOR THOSE WHO
WANT TO SEE THEM.

Henri Matisse

SPEAK OR ACT
WITH A PURE MIND
AND HAPPINESS WILL
FOLLOW YOU AS
YOUR SHADOW.

Buddha

WHAT MAKES THE
DESERT BEAUTIFUL...
IS THAT SOMEWHERE
IT HIDES A WELL.

Antoine de Saint-Exupéry

MAKE TIME FOR THE THINGS THAT MATTER

The busier we get, the more we put other aspects of our lives on hold. An important contribution to our happiness is the time we spend with close family and good friends, so make the effort and plan a get-together, even if it's just a cup of tea and a catch-up.

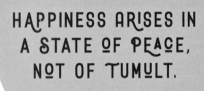

HAPPINESS ARISES IN
A STATE OF PEACE,
NOT OF TUMULT.

Ann Radcliffe

YOU'RE THE
BLACKSMITH OF YOUR
OWN HAPPINESS.

Swedish proverb

DON'T FORGET HOW GREAT YOU ARE!

Beware of self-critical thoughts. Low levels of self-esteem correlate to lower feelings of happiness, so try to put things into perspective. Build up your sense of appreciation for the positive skills and attributes you possess and recognize the blessings around you in life.

ACT THE WAY YOU
WANT TO FEEL.

Gretchen Rubin

TO BE WITHOUT SOME OF
THE THINGS YOU WANT
IS AN INDISPENSABLE
PART OF HAPPINESS.

Bertrand Russell

DEAL WITH WHAT'S WORRYING YOU

Sometimes chores remain in the back of our minds, waiting to get done. It could be checking out prices of electricity suppliers, renewing a magazine subscription or making an overdue dental appointment. For an instant happiness rush, deal with it now.

FALL DOWN
SEVEN TIMES,
STAND UP EIGHT.

Japanese proverb

KEEPING BUSY AND MAKING
OPTIMISM A WAY OF
LIFE CAN RESTORE YOUR
FAITH IN YOURSELF.

Lucille Ball

LISTEN TO ALL YOUR SENSES

Slow down and pay attention to your
surroundings. Use all your senses
to enjoy your current environment,
and before moving on, get your next
destination clear in your mind.

ONCE YOU REPLACE
NEGATIVE THOUGHTS
WITH POSITIVE ONES,
YOU'LL START HAVING
POSITIVE RESULTS.

Willie Nelson

BE IN LOVE
WITH YOUR LIFE.
EVERY MINUTE
OF IT.

Jack Kerouac

ENJOY DOING THINGS WELL

Find the little things you're good at and give credit to yourself for each of them – no matter how insignificant you might deem them to be. You don't have to strive to be the world's greatest at anything in order to be happy – doing everything to the best of your ability is enough!

ONE MAY WALK OVER
THE HIGHEST MOUNTAIN
ONE STEP AT A TIME.

John Wanamaker

IF YOU ASK ME
WHAT I CAME INTO THIS
LIFE TO DO, I WILL
TELL YOU: I CAME TO
LIVE OUT LOUD.

Émile Zola

LIVE IN A JOYFUL NETWORK

Research shows that our happiness not only flourishes with those in our direct social network, such as neighbours, friends and family, but is influenced by the people our friends know too. So joyfulness echoes out through groups of people, like a radar system. Keep in contact and spread the joy!

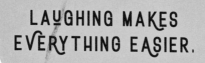

LAUGHING MAKES
EVERYTHING EASIER.

Carmen Electra

CHEERFULNESS IS THE VERY FLOWER OF HEALTH.

Proverb

TAKE STEPS TO HAPPINESS

Walking is one of the most effective ways to replenish your inner joy, so incorporate a short walk into your daily routine if you can. The more you walk, the more you'll see – and you'll soon find yourself looking forward to taking to the pavements, in all weathers!

FOLKS ARE USUALLY
ABOUT AS HAPPY AS
THEY MAKE UP THEIR
MINDS TO BE.

Anonymous

FIND ECSTASY IN LIFE;
THE MERE SENSE OF
LIVING IS JOY ENOUGH.

Emily Dickinson

HAPPY SNACKING

Have you noticed that when you feel low, you often have cravings for foods containing refined sugar, like chocolate and cake? This is your body's way of getting a quick fix of happiness, because eating sugar produces insulin which elicits a temporary feeling of elation. Better food choices to improve your mood would be those rich in vitamin B6, such as spinach and salmon, and magnesium-rich foods like bananas and oat bran.

YOU ARE NEVER TOO OLD
TO SET ANOTHER GOAL OR
TO DREAM A NEW DREAM.

Les Brown

WE ARE ALL IN THE
GUTTER, BUT SOME
OF US ARE LOOKING
AT THE STARS.

Oscar Wilde

EXPERIENCE THE NATURAL WORLD

Sometimes we need to make time to be in awe of life. Stand on the top of a mountain or hill, or look up at an expanse of night sky in the wilderness. Happiness comes from our sense of being connected to others and the world around us.

LAUGH AND THE WORLD
LAUGHS WITH YOU.

Ella Wheeler Wilcox

IT'S ALWAYS TOO
EARLY TO QUIT.

Norman Vincent Peale

HOME SWEET HOME

Love the place you live. Sometimes being away reminds us how fond of home we really are. Look with renewed eyes on your home and appreciate everything your area has to offer.

HAPPINESS IS
THE BEST MAKE-UP;
A SMILE IS BETTER
THAN ANY LIPSTICK
YOU'LL PUT ON.

Drew Barrymore

IF YOU WANT YOUR
LIFE TO BE A MAGNIFICENT
STORY, THEN BEGIN BY
REALIZING THAT YOU
ARE THE AUTHOR.

Mark Houlahan

YOU ARE NOT YOUR EMOTIONS

When a strong emotion arises – such as anger, hurt or fear – allow yourself to pause before you react. Notice your breath and the sensations in your body. You may then recognize that you have a choice about what you do next.

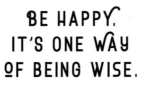

BE HAPPY.
IT'S ONE WAY
OF BEING WISE.

Colette

HAPPINESS IS WHEN WHAT YOU THINK, WHAT YOU SAY, AND WHAT YOU DO ARE IN HARMONY.

Mahatma Gandhi

IT'S A VISION THING

Create a "vision board" collage which depicts what goals and priorities you want to focus on in your life. Keep your vision board in view so that you can frequently look at it and remind yourself of the happy direction your life is taking.

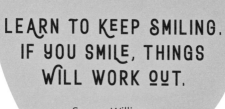

LEARN TO KEEP SMILING.
IF YOU SMILE, THINGS
WILL WORK OUT.

Serena Williams

MAY YOU LIVE EVERY DAY OF YOUR LIFE.

Jonathan Swift

OLDER AND WISER

As we get older, we often become happier. With maturing years, we better appreciate the true value of family and friends, which makes us feel more content. Our brains also contain increased levels of the chemicals that enable us to feel stable and sanguine. Let's raise a toast to our elder years!

THE IMPORTANT THING...
IS NOT HOW MANY YEARS
IN YOUR LIFE, BUT HOW
MUCH LIFE IN YOUR YEARS!

Edward Stieglitz

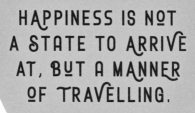

HAPPINESS IS NOT
A STATE TO ARRIVE
AT, BUT A MANNER
OF TRAVELLING.

Margaret Lee Runbeck

IF YOU'RE NOT HAPPY,
YOU CAN BECOME
HAPPY. HAPPINESS
IS A CHOICE.

Jennifer Aniston

A COMFORTABLE NEST
TO COME HOME TO

If you are redecorating your home,
consider the colours that elicit a happy
response for you. Everyone has different
tastes, so choose colours that are
calming yet uplifting. As a result, you
will feel more positive about returning
home to your joyful surroundings.

TO SUCCEED IN LIFE,
YOU NEED THREE THINGS:
A WISHBONE, A BACKBONE
AND A FUNNY BONE.

Reba McEntire

HAPPINESS CONSISTS
NOT IN HAVING MUCH,
BUT IN BEING CONTENT
WITH LITTLE.

Marguerite Gardiner

SPREAD A LITTLE HAPPINESS

It really is true – by helping others, we feel happier. It's a great exchange for a little bit of your time each week. Check out your local charities to see how you can get involved and volunteer.

IF YOU HAVE
A GARDEN AND A
LIBRARY, YOU HAVE
EVERYTHING
YOU NEED.

Cicero

LOOK AT EVERYTHING
AS THOUGH YOU WERE
SEEING IT FOR THE
FIRST OR LAST TIME.

Betty Smith

THINK POSITIVE

If you experience the noise of negative chatter in your mind, remember that it is a sign you need to attune to a positive, happier state. Take a moment to sit with yourself. Think of all the things you like about yourself – perhaps you're super kind, you're good at making people smile, or you're a great problem-solver. Then think about the amazing things you can do – what are your talents, passions and skills? These are the things about yourself that you should be paying attention to!

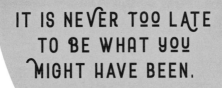

IT IS NEVER TOO LATE
TO BE WHAT YOU
MIGHT HAVE BEEN.

Adelaide Anne Proctor

THE FOOLISH MAN
SEEKS HAPPINESS IN THE
DISTANCE, THE WISE
GROWS IT UNDER HIS FEET.

James Oppenheim

IF YOU WANT
TO BE HAPPY, BE.

Leo Tolstoy

SWITCH OFF AND TUNE IN

Take time to unplug from technology. If you're waiting in a queue, resist the urge to check texts and emails on your phone. Take notice of your posture and adjust it to be comfortable. Focus on your breathing while you wait, remaining calm and undisturbed.

LAUGHTER IS THE
SOUND OF THE
SOUL DANCING.

Jarod Kintz

WHOEVER IS HAPPY WILL
MAKE OTHERS HAPPY TOO.

Anne Frank

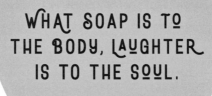

WHAT SOAP IS TO
THE BODY, LAUGHTER
IS TO THE SOUL.

Yiddish proverb

CHOOSE WISELY

It is said in Native American lore that there are two wolves within your heart. You can feed the wolf of love and happiness or the wolf of hate and ill-will – whichever one you feed will grow.

BE CONTENT WITH WHAT
YOU HAVE... WHEN YOU
REALIZE THERE IS NOTHING
LACKING, THE WHOLE
WORLD BELONGS TO YOU.

Lao Tzu

A TABLE, A CHAIR,
A BOWL OF FRUIT
AND A VIOLIN; WHAT
ELSE DOES A MAN
NEED TO BE HAPPY?

Albert Einstein

INSPIRE YOURSELF EVERY DAY

Do you find yourself thinking things like "I'm not clever enough" or "I'm never going to be good at this?" If so, it's time to press the delete button on negative self-talk and replace it with positive. Write down some inspiring phrases and read them to yourself daily.

ALL LIFE IS AN EXPERIMENT.
THE MORE EXPERIMENTS
YOU MAKE, THE BETTER.

Ralph Waldo Emerson

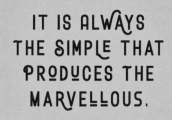

IT IS ALWAYS
THE SIMPLE THAT
PRODUCES THE
MARVELLOUS.

Amelia Barr

BUILD AN INSPIRATIONAL LIBRARY

Keep some of your favourite pieces of
writing close to hand, so that you can
refer to them when you feel yourself
slipping toward negativity. Poems, prayers,
song lyrics or phrases from a favourite
novel can all replenish and inspire.

OPTIMISM IS A HAPPINESS
MAGNET. IF YOU STAY
POSITIVE, GOOD THINGS
AND GOOD PEOPLE WILL
BE DRAWN TO YOU.

Mary Lou Retton

IT'S NEVER TOO
LATE TO HAVE A
HAPPY CHILDHOOD.

Wayne Dyer

GIVE CBT A CHANCE

If you find yourself excessively worrying about things, it may be worth trying some cognitive behavioural therapy (CBT). This is a brief, one-to-one treatment to help you notice when you are worrying, break the habit and then implement alternative ways of reacting to your everyday problems.

THOSE WHO BRING
SUNSHINE INTO THE LIVES
OF OTHERS CANNOT KEEP
IT FROM THEMSELVES.

J. M. Barrie

EVERY DAY BRINGS A
CHANCE FOR YOU TO DRAW
IN A BREATH, KICK OFF
YOUR SHOES... AND DANCE.

Oprah Winfrey

SMILE INSIDE

Try an internal smile – think of something that makes you happy and experience the warm smiling feeling within. You can tap into this internal smile whenever you wish.

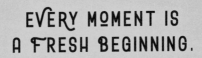

EVERY MOMENT IS
A FRESH BEGINNING.

T. S. Eliot

HAPPINESS IS
SOMETHING THAT COMES
INTO OUR LIVES THROUGH
DOORS WE DON'T EVEN
REMEMBER LEAVING OPEN.

Rose Wilder Lane

DOING IS BETTER THAN HAVING

Spending your money on "experiences" – like eating out and travelling to new or favourite places – rather than on expensive items can be very rewarding. Research indicates we gain more happiness from our memories than from material things, so consider this next time you reach for your purse or wallet.

ANGELS CAN FLY
BECAUSE THEY TAKE
THEMSELVES LIGHTLY.

G. K. Chesterton

IT'S NEVER TOO LATE
– NEVER TOO LATE TO
START OVER, NEVER TOO
LATE TO BE HAPPY.

Jane Fonda

TRANSMIT YOUR HAPPY THOUGHTS

Share your own happiness by sending joyful thoughts to someone who is feeling sad or unwell. Simply bring them to mind and imagine you are directing loving wishes toward them, to arrive even faster than special delivery.

LIFE ISN'T ABOUT
WAITING FOR THE
STORM TO PASS; IT'S
ABOUT LEARNING TO
DANCE IN THE RAIN.

Anonymous

WHAT WE SEE DEPENDS MAINLY ON WHAT WE LOOK FOR.

John Lubbock

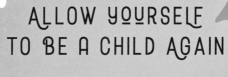

ALLOW YOURSELF
TO BE A CHILD AGAIN

Do you remember how things
seemed magical when you were
a child? Look out for moments of
enchantment, courtesy of nature:
a rainbow, shimmering raindrops
on tree branches or a bird singing.
Allow yourself to cherish these
glimpses of wonder in your heart.

HAPPINESS, NOT IN
ANOTHER PLACE BUT
THIS PLACE, NOT
FOR ANOTHER HOUR
BUT THIS HOUR.

Walt Whitman

LAUGHTER IS A SUNBEAM
OF THE SOUL.

Thomas Mann

WRITE DOWN
YOUR GOALS

Create an "action list". Base on it
things you have been meaning to try,
future goals for your work and ideas
for spending time with friends and
family. Look over it now and again to
remind you of life's possibilities and
to nudge you into new directions.

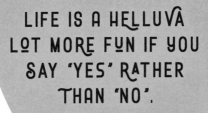

LIFE IS A HELLUVA LOT MORE FUN IF YOU SAY 'YES' RATHER THAN 'NO'.

Richard Branson

YOU WILL NEVER BE
HAPPIER THAN YOU
EXPECT. TO CHANGE
YOUR HAPPINESS, CHANGE
YOUR EXPECTATION.

Bette Davis

CELEBRATE WHENEVER YOU CAN!

There are many opportunities to share happiness and gratitude: the completion of a big work project, the all-clear with a health issue, the start of something new. All of life's stepping stones deserve joyful acknowledgement.

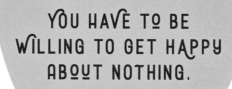

YOU HAVE TO BE
WILLING TO GET HAPPY
ABOUT NOTHING.

Andy Warhol

LOVE IS THE
ENERGY OF LIFE.

Robert Browning

TAKE TIME TO MAKE OTHER PEOPLE HAPPY

Think about how you can create
more happiness for others. Thinking
and planning something special for
another person can be as enjoyable and
fulfilling as the recipient's experience.

WE'RE ALL GOLDEN
SUNFLOWERS INSIDE.

Allen Ginsberg

NEVER DULL YOUR SHINE FOR SOMEBODY ELSE.

Tyra Banks

CONSIDER A CAREER CHANGE

Many people are now choosing happiness by developing a "lifestyle business". This is where you work on something you are passionate about and that allows you to be flexible when it comes to your workspace and hours. It can be started alongside your paid job and quite often works well with child-rearing. So be creative and think outside the box to manifest the work-life balance that you really want.

THE SMALL HAPPY
MOMENTS ADD UP.
A LITTLE BIT OF JOY
GOES A LONG WAY.

Melissa McCarthy

GIVE OUT WHAT
YOU MOST WANT
TO COME BACK.

Robin Sharma

GO WITH THE FLOW

Be flexible and let go of fixed expectations. This gives you the opportunity to embrace whatever comes your way and means that you're less likely to be disappointed if things don't turn out the way you planned. *C'est la vie!*

JUST BELIEVE IN
YOURSELF. EVEN IF YOU
DON'T, PRETEND THAT
YOU DO AND, AT SOME
POINT, YOU WILL.

Venus Williams

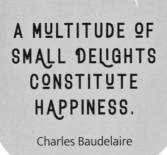

A MULTITUDE OF
SMALL DELIGHTS
CONSTITUTE
HAPPINESS.

Charles Baudelaire

REMEMBER, HAPPINESS DOESN'T DEPEND UPON WHO YOU ARE OR WHAT YOU HAVE; IT DEPENDS SOLELY UPON WHAT YOU THINK.

Dale Carnegie

DO ANYTHING, BUT LET IT PRODUCE JOY.

Henry Miller

If you're interested in finding out more about our books, find us on Facebook at **Summersdale Publishers** and follow us on Twitter at **@Summersdale**.

www.summersdale.com